Getting Organized at Work

"I'm amazed at how many time management courses talk about the ability to change time and reality. I say rather, 'Embrace reality and see what you can do to take advantage of it.'"

"The key is action. Pick the ideas
and strategies that apply to you.
Then take action and make them work!"

Getting Organized at Work

✔ 24 Lessons to Set Goals, Establish Priorities, and Manage Your Time

KENNETH ZEIGLER

New York Chicago San Francisco Lisbon
London Madrid Mexico City Milan New Delhi
San Juan Seoul Singapore Sydney Toronto

3 4 5 6 7 8 9 0 DOC/DOC 1 5 4 3 2 1 0

ISBN: 978-0-07-159138-6
MHID: 0-07-159138-9

This publication is designed to provide accurate and authoritative information in regard to the subject matter covered. It is sold with the understanding that the publisher is not engaged in rendering legal, accounting, or other professional service. If legal advice or other expert assistance is required, the services of a competent professional person should be sought.

—*From a Declaration of Principles Jointly Adopted by a Committee of the American Bar Association and a Committee of Publishers and Associations*

McGraw-Hill books are available at special quantity discounts to use as premiums and sales promotions, or for use in corporate training programs. To contact a representative, please visit the Contact Us pages at www.mhprofessional.com.

This book is printed on acid-free paper.

Contents

Getting Organized at Work

☑ Organize for success!

The goal of this book is to provide tips, tools, ideas, and strategies that you can apply and see immediate, measurable improvement, both at work and at home. This book will help you use whatever system you're currently using more effectively.

Many time management courses talk about the ability to change time and reality. That seems impractical. Instead of acting like the salmon and swimming against the current, go with the flow—but add structure and discipline.

This book is intended to get you to analyze your use of time and answer this question: *Why* are you doing *what* you're doing *when* you're doing it?

Follow these three steps:

1. Keep track of your time (work and personal) for a week. It may surprise you to find out how much time tasks and activities take.

2. Then, analyze your findings. Identify any activities that are unnecessary and eliminate them.

3. Find or create times that you could block off for important tasks or activities that have a high pay-off. Sometimes these tasks and activities get delayed because of things that are relatively less important or even unnecessary.

Once you keep track of your time for a week, you should see patterns in activities, tasks, interruptions, and unplanned events. Once you see those patterns, use the strategies discussed in this book to handle them more effectively.

The key is action. Pick two or three ideas or strategies at a time and work on them until they become a habit. Then pick two or three more and work on them until they become a habit. At the end of every week, ask yourself what you could do better next week. In addition, realize that there are two aspects to saving time:

- Improving your time management skills
- Training others so their time management skills don't interfere with yours.

"This book is for anyone who would like to become more efficient, get more done in less time, and have balance in life."

☐ ~~Let events rule~~

☑ **Take control of your day**

Do you ever feel like you get to work and your day takes control of you? You must become more "proactive" and less "reactive" to become the "Ringmaster" instead of the beast. The Ringmaster is very patient and consistent, and has discipline. Here are *seven strategies* to take control of your day:

Slow down: You're moving so fast that it takes multiple phone calls, e-mails, and meetings to accomplish the same thing we used to be able to do more simply. The Ringmaster tries to send an e-mail only once, make this call once, and/or have this meeting once. In order to do this, you would have to plan your call before you pick up the phone, plan your e-mail before you start typing, and prepare and give out an agenda well in advance of your meeting.

Stop doing everything immediately: The single most counterproductive event you experience daily is doing everything the second someone asks or you think of it. Start negotiating new requests so they fit better into your day, but still work for the requestor. This will improve the number of tasks you are completing daily.

Cut down on relationship building: When you get into a groove first thing in the morning and a coworker stops by to chat, the Ringmaster suggests talking at break time or at lunch, when it's most appropriate.

The Ringmaster realized that relationship building was all about quality, not quantity. If you set aside time each day to share with and listen to others, the quality of your working relationships would actually improve.

Batch like tasks or activities: The Ringmaster sets up times each day to work on like activities he or she has to accomplish to have more DISCIPLINE. The Ringmaster tries to answer e-mail, say, four times a day and turns off the audible notification. By only answering e-mails, each e-mail will take less time because you are basically replicating the same activity over and over. Now return phone calls. Finally go see your direct reports and see if they need any help or answers to questions.

Direct the request to the right person: Are you a people pleaser? When the Ringmaster gets a request that is not in his or her area of expertise, he or she directs the requestor to the right person. It is faster for the right person to answer the question or solve the problem than it is for you to try to do it! Focus on making sure you get your required work out of the way; otherwise, it will be left until the end of the day.

Improve the way you communicate: One of the fastest ways to improve productivity is to be more specific and detailed with others. This will save time for you, your direct reports, and others. This really eliminates questions and misunderstandings. Stop using "ASAP" immediately! You must improve the way you communicate first. Could you eliminate simple questions by being more specific?

Do one thing at a time, like successful people do: Try to bring 100 percent of your focus and concentration to bear on one activity. Tasks will take less time to complete and you'll make fewer mistakes. Either choose the phone call or the e-mail message, and put off the other until you've finished the one you chose. It's not about how many tasks you start in a day, it's about how many you complete.

"To become a ringmaster, you must realize that there's a time and a place for everything. Successful time managers realize that it's all about discipline."

☐ ~~Do everything yourself~~

☑ **Train others**

The most sought-after management skill today is the ability to train others, including your peers and direct reports. Training is such a difficult skill because it takes time and effort to be truly successful.

The Ringmaster realized a long time ago that even if he or she had excellent time management skills, his or her coworkers and direct reports would still make life difficult with their poor time management skills. Here are four suggestions:

Problem solving and questions: When direct reports or peers come to you with a problem or question, you should realize it is a training opportunity in disguise. (If you answer their questions or solve their problems quickly, they will be back again, usually asking roughly the same questions.) Ask them to:

- Clearly identify their problem or question
- Explain what they have already tried

■ Tell you what they think the answer is.

Offer to show them how to do it so they really learn something from your answer. People like to learn new things, but it takes time (i.e., training) to save time.

Train others to use the phone and voice mail: The Ringmaster changes his or her voice mail greeting daily or weekly and asks callers to leave their name, number, reason for the call, and the best time to call them back. He or she explains that if they do that, he or she will call them back more quickly with the help or information the requestor needs and leave it on their voice mail. This strategy will also cut down on "phone tag."

You must lead by example. When you leave messages for others, you must leave the same type of information as you ask from them. If you don't do what you're asking others to do for you, why should they? Train your direct reports to change their voice mail regularly and tell them how to leave a voice mail you can quickly respond to.

Train others to write you better e-mails: Ask others to put the reason they're sending an e-mail to you in the subject line and what they want and when they specifically need it in the first three lines of the message. Explain if they did that you could respond faster to their e-mail messages. Make sure to show your direct reports on how to write you e-mails that you will respond to (by being brief and to the point).

You need to write your e-mails this way for others first and be an example. In addition, use bullets and numbers instead of long paragraphs and ask them to do the same. It will "invite" your readers to read your messages faster.

Train others in how to communicate better: E-mail is for information, whereas phone calls and meetings are for discussion. When you see e-mails from your direct reports going back and forth, ask them to stop and schedule time to talk. Have you been to a meeting and didn't say anything? Maybe you should have suggested that they send you the minutes via e-mail.

"The most sought-after management skill today is the ability to train others. The Ringmaster is a great trainer because he or she leads by example."

☐ ~~Postpone starting~~

☑ Get projects done

The first step in project management is to define your desired end result or outcome. This is the end result toward which you direct time, energy, and resources. If you are receiving a project from someone else, be sure to ask a lot of questions to be sure exactly what their expectations are. Now write it down. If you are giving a project to someone else, be sure to be specific as to what your expectations are!

Here are the two enemies that prevent us from doing the right thing:

Enemy #1: Working on everything but your project: Today we are so focused on putting out the fires that progress toward finishing our projects on time is very slow or nonexistent. If your activity doesn't contribute directly toward completing a project, you may be wasting your time. Remember: putting out fires just helps maintain the status quo. If you solve the cause of the fire and fix it, that's something that improves the company and will get you noticed.

You must put your project plan into your calendar first, because these projects are the highest priority. Otherwise, your daily, weekly, and monthly plans won't be as effective as they could be.

Enemy #2: Procrastination: Because projects are often very large with long time frames for accomplishing them, we often procrastinate before starting them. Your next tip will help you overcome this enemy every time.

Have a clear vision of what is expected of you: Make sure you know exactly what the desired end result of your projects needs to be. It's faster to ask questions and be 100 percent right than to start with little or no information and have to do it all over again. This will also allow you to prioritize your work more accurately.

Brainstorm: As you look at your desired end result, write down whatever pops into your head in no particular order. Some questions to consider are:

- Who are you going to need to help you? Are they available?
- What information do you need and who has it?
- What could go wrong and how are you going to overcome it? (What has gone wrong in the past?)

■ What are my ideas about this project?

By brainstorming you are breaking your project down into manageable steps. This will cut down on the chances you will procrastinate working on your project.

The mind is a great organizer. When it can see everything you need to do, it will group them together and set up batching to speed its completion. There is a direct correlation between how much you write down and the probability of completing your project on time. And because we're visual, seeing your words makes your commitment more obvious.

Write down a start and completion date: Writing down a specific start and completion date will increase your focus and the likelihood of completing your project on time. If you don't get one when you are given the project, ask for one.

If you are the one assigning the project, make sure you tell your direct report or reports exactly when you expect the project to be completed. This will help them prioritize your request and eliminate confusion.

"You've got to be careful if you don't know where you're going, because you might not get there."

—Yogi Berra

☐ ~~Just be optimistic~~

☑ **Think realistically**

What's the number one reason why people don't complete their projects on time? It's because they haven't left any room for anything to go wrong, such as interruptions or unexpected problems.

That's why it's so important to try to anticipate potential obstacles or changes from the start or at least before they occur. That's also why it's important to review your progress constantly and check with team members. Identify any problems as early as possible and devise a plan to avoid or resolve each problem.

When someone gives you a project, ask as many questions as necessary at the start, to understand the project and determine what's expected as well as is possible.

When you allow room in your plan for things to go wrong, you can be more confident that you'll meet your deadlines and achieve your goals. Then, you can be optimistic—realistically.

Believe you can meet your deadline: In order to complete a project on time, it's important to believe that you can do it. Make sure your deadline is achievable and your time frame is realistic. It's better to underpromise and overdeliver than to overpromise and underdeliver.

If you don't believe your deadline is realistic and achievable, be sure you can prove why. Be prepared to offer a solution that is realistic, and to explain why. No one likes a complainer. People like a solution provider.

Identify who you're going to need: Before you begin, be sure you write down in your plan who you're going to need help from and when. Check with them to see if they have the time to help and if your expectations and assumptions are correct before you begin!

Identify what could go wrong: As you are putting together your plan, consider this. Have I done anything like this is the past and what went wrong? The past is an excellent indicator of the future. Now leave room in your plan for things to go wrong. Usually very few things go wrong when you do this. What is the result? You'll finish early or, worst case, on time.

"Have a clear vision of what's important to your leader. Make sure you know exactly what he or she wants the end result to be or look like. It's faster to ask questions and be 100 percent right than to start with little or no information and have to do it all over again."

☐ ~~Start now~~

☑ **Plan your work**

Before you start your project, there are three more tips we need to go over so you'll be sure to succeed:

Identify when you're going to work on your project: Ask yourself, "When, during the course of each day or week, am I going to work on my part of my project? What is the best block of time to reserve so I can spend quality time working on my project? Can I start it first thing in the morning so I can get it out of the way and so it isn't left on my list at the end of the day?" The best time to work on your project is when you typically get the fewest interruptions.

By doing this, you'll increase the chance of success. First, you'll be putting your project into your schedule at a specific time, so that you don't put it off to the end of the day; second, you'll be making a commitment; and third, you'll be using clear thought to pick the correct time to work on it.

Make your weekly/monthly results measurable: When you set up your project, identify how much you need to accomplish daily and in many cases weekly to achieve your deadline on time. Each Friday afternoon you can measure whether you are on schedule or need to make adjustments the next week.

I see more people give up because they didn't get to where they wanted to be by the end of the first week. Remember, though, that when you first set up the project, you were making assumptions based on limited information.

Cure: Stay flexible and anticipate that you're going to have to make adjustments at the end of each week so you won't get so discouraged. That's why you have to build extra time into your plan.

Create rewards for each step of the project: Success should be rewarded. So, you should set a reward for succeeding in each step of a project, proportionate to the importance of the step. The reward doesn't have to cost money. Your reward should at least improve the quality of your personal life. Your reward should be something you could look forward to. Don't make it something you'd give yourself anyway.

"A plan without action is a daydream; action without a plan is a nightmare."

—Japanese proverb

☐ ~~Put it off~~

☑ Don't procrastinate

The number one way to overcome procrastination is to break down a project and work on it a little every day. But sometimes even the best planning isn't enough to overcome a basic human tendency. We all procrastinate to some degree and in some ways. That's why we must do the following:

- Realize when we're procrastinating and understand why.
- Identify the activities that we prefer to the tasks that we're avoiding.
- Determine steps to manage and overcome our procrastination.

Why do you procrastinate? Do any of the following thoughts seem familiar?

The task is unpleasant. The task is difficult. I'm overwhelmed: too many tasks. I'm interrupted too often. I'm not organized enough. I don't have the necessary information. I don't have clear or written goals. I'm not in the mood. I'm not interested in the task. I don't have time now. I don't have the energy now. This isn't due for a while.

What activities take you from the tasks that you put off? You may have some favorites—and your reasons may be keeping you from making the most of your potential. Take a moment to list the activities that you prefer to do when you have tasks scheduled. You may learn some interesting things about yourself.

Here are three tips to escape the tendency to procrastinate:

Work on the tasks in the morning: You probably have more energy and can focus better at that time. It's tempting to handle all of the urgent matters and then, after you've put out the fires, to turn to the tasks you've scheduled. That's probably the worst time to do them—if you get to them at all.

Break down your work into smaller parts: A human tendency is to start tasks that we perceive take short amounts of time. The number one way to overcome procrastination is to break your larger task into smaller ones that take about 20–30 minutes to complete. By completing smaller tasks, you'll build confidence to get the job done. Remember: if the task looks easy and won't take much time, human nature will cause you to choose that task before others

Cut down on interruptions: Interruptions derail us from getting things done. Try to limit interruptions so you can bring 100 percent focus and concentration on that "veggie." One hour of uninterrupted time is like four "typical" hours you're currently experiencing. Here are some strategies to help you:

- Block out time each day on your computer to get your veggies done.
- Defer the interruption by negotiating a better time for the activity.
- Let the phone call go to voice mail.
- Turn off your e-mail notification so you can't see or hear it.

Reward yourself: Before you start that difficult or unpleasant task, think of a way to reward yourself when you complete it. People talk about improving the quality of their personal lives. Why not start by giving yourself mini-rewards that improve the quality of your personal life? Of course, you can always wait and hope until the end of the year!

"Procrastination makes easy things hard, hard things harder."

—Mason Cooley

☐ ~~Go with the flow~~

☑ **Organize your work**

Now that you've learned to control your day more effectively and plan your projects, it will be important to develop a system to keep track of everything that's bombarding you from all sides. This lesson will show you why it's so important to write more down—then how to organize it effectively—so you get more accomplished each day.

Instead of using your mind as a "memory chip" your mind would be much more effective if you turned it into a high powered "processor." The mind is a great organizer when it isn't bogged down trying to remember everything you need to do, both at work and home.

The Master List recommended here is a hybrid of a traditional to-do list.

In brief, a Master List is a pad of paper where you will keep all the possible activities, notes, action items, etc., for an entire week. It is used in combination with a Daily List (a paper or electronic calendar). Here's how to keep a Master List:

1. Only have one list: A Master List replaces everything else you are using—i.e., Post-it® notes, etc. It is a pad of paper versus a piece of paper. It should be a pad you will take with you wherever you go because your mind is always thinking of tasks and ideas. Your work and personal life all go together in one place, on your Master List. That way you only have to look in one place for to-dos, etc. The average person loses 45 minutes a day looking for things. If organizing takes too long you will stop doing it.

2. As thoughts pop into your head, write them down: The purpose of a Master List is to keep your mind empty. This ensures that you don't lose any ideas and increase your focus and concentration. If you don't have your Master List handy, leave a message on your voice mail.

This will help you think ahead because a traditional to-do list only focuses on the activities you need to do that day or the next day. Now you will be writing down tasks and ideas that need to be completed days and/or weeks from now.

3. Skip lines between entries: This way you can make notes and it doesn't get cluttered. You should be able to find and read items easily, when you need them or when you're transferring items to your calendar. The first word of each entry should tell you what it is—i.e., e-mail, call, to-do.

4. Only rewrite your Master List once a week: Each Friday you will begin a new Master List and only transfer those items you didn't complete that week. Why should you have to rewrite it every day?

5. Save your Master List until the end of the year: After you write your new Master List, take your old one, staple and file it to use as "back-up" or reference to jog your memory and referred to for your annual review. Why not get the credit you deserve on your review?

6. Don't prioritize your Master List: Since your day and priorities are constantly changing, your list needs to be very flexible. Sometimes you won't necessarily choose a task based on priority but rather by how long it takes so it fits the time you have available.

7. The first word on each line defines the task: When you go to "batch" like tasks just look along the margin at the first word, (i.e., e-mail, call, to-do.) Details will save time and prevent misunderstandings. Be sure to make notes from phone conversations, meetings, and to-dos you agree to at a later time. Now add your personal to-dos to your list so you don't forget to have a personal life.

"It is more important to know where you are going than to get there quickly. Do not mistake activity for achievement."

—Mabel Newcomber

☐ ~~Don't look ahead~~

☑ **Add closure daily**

A Master List is updated at the end of each day. Fifteen minutes before you plan to leave work, stop responding to e-mails, phone calls, requests from others, and your work. This is your time. With your calendar open and your Master List in front of you, let your mind wander. Brainstorm: write down whatever pops into your head in particular order. Why do it at the end of every day? Here are some reasons:

■ Closure (the mind wants to be in control at the end of the day)

■ Mental separation between work and home

■ Time and a place for everything. Organizational skills don't take a lot of energy. They're perfect at the end of the day. When you're fresh first thing each day you shouldn't be organizing.

■ How can you have a quality personal life when you're taking work home mentally? We need to turn the lights off mentally when we leave work.

- To increase productivity first thing each day, you should be "fresh" because you "recharged" the night before. If you are tired first thing in the morning you have a high probability of getting "bogged" down in e-mail or "relationship building."

- When you are fresh and focused first thing in the morning, you don't want to spend that time organizing. You want to spend it working on the most difficult task on your list.

- People are more confident and look forward to coming to work when they have a "plan" from the night before.

When you get to work the next day add new tasks to the end of your existing Master List, pick the most important one and get started.

Review your Master List throughout the day: Each time you complete a task, come back and look at your Master List to decide on the next task to work on. Before you commit to doing a new request, make sure it doesn't conflict with something already on your list.

Not everything will get crossed off your list: Accept the reality that you won't be crossing off every item on your Master List by the end of the day. Reduce the pressure. Don't work late: there's no correlation in productivity between the length of the day and the amount of work accomplished.

Use Friday afternoons to improve: When you rewrite your Master List each Friday, you can evaluate your performance. When you transfer an item not yet completed to a new Master List, ask yourself.

- What was the priority of the task?
- Why didn't I get it done?
- What am I going to do different next week to get it done?

Keep your list handy at all times: With your Master List in hand, you're less likely to try to handle the request immediately. Look at your list and schedule the request appropriately. That's how you develop discipline in your time management.

Be sure you add personal balance to your list: If you don't balance your work with your personal life, it will affect your productivity. Try not to have separate lists for each. I didn't get a personal life until I started writing it down and could see check marks next to personal tasks and/or activities.

"People ask me how I got good at managing my time. One week at a time. Each Friday afternoon I look over what I've accomplished for the week and consider what I could do better the next week and where I could save time."

☐ ~~Do what's easiest first~~

☑ Use the "veggie" principle daily

Now that you know how to use a Master List, it's time to use that list to get more accomplished daily, weekly, and monthly. We are going to examine a "typical" day and how to develop strategies to get more accomplished in less time so you can have better work/life balance. The place to start is with how to apply the Veggie Principle to get off to a faster start each day and get more accomplished in the first half of your workday.

The Veggie Principle and how to apply it: A "veggie" is a task, activity, or project that's good for you and your career or personal life, but that you have a hard time "eating," or doing first. Without the benefit of training such as this, people will typically start working on a veggie late in the day or evening when they are less effective.

The true secret to getting what matters most accomplished each day is to apply the "veggie principle," that is, tackle first in the day those action items that directly impact your highest goals and priorities.

Your "veggies" will take less time in the morning because you have more energy in the morning. It's your peak energy cycle, you'll have more focus, and you'll have more confidence/feel great by getting them out of the way first thing. This will also dramatically cut down on procrastination.

Making an effective Daily List: Use your Master List, a day planner, or an electronic calendar to make a Daily List. Here's how to make and use your Daily List:

- At the end of the day, select two to six tasks from your Master List and put them onto your calendar for tomorrow. Leave room for the next morning.
- The next morning add another two or three "veggie" e-mails and/or voice mails to your day. Altogether, your day is full. (A "veggie" e-mail or voice mail has a specific deadline to be done right away, and it explains why it's important.)

Then, identify the two biggest "veggies" on your list and commit to making sure they get accomplished today. Typically, the top two will give you 80 percent of the value of all of the tasks listed. Build your day around these two tasks and try to "sprinkle" the "fires" around them so you will accomplish them.

Try to start the morning with one of them and complete the other before lunch. If you put them off until the afternoon, they might not get done at all and probably will be put off until tomorrow.

Take breaks between tasks: If you take a few moments to refresh yourself and shift gears after each task, you can work more productively. In addition, be sure to take lunch so you can recharge and make better use of your afternoon cycle.

Use Friday afternoon to organize next week more effectively: Friday afternoon is the lowest productivity time of the week, perfect for organizing. Every Friday afternoon you should:

■ Make a new Master List by transferring the tasks and activities you weren't able to complete that week to your new list. Now add anything else that comes to mind.
■ Delete and file e-mails and papers.
■ Create mental separation between work and home.

"There is no correlation between how long you sit at your desk and what you accomplish."

☐ ~~Make a to-do list~~

☑ Plan for power

At the end of the day when you schedule your next day, plan a powerful morning. The average person starts the day by spending one to three hours taking care of e-mail, voice mail, and phone calls and checking in with the boss and others—"relationship building." Reduce this to 15 to 30 minutes so you can get to your first "veggie" sooner.

Check your e-mail and voice mail for "veggies" only. Add them to your list. Then, close your e-mail and turn off the notification, put your phone on voice mail, and jump into your list.

Devote an hour to your biggest "veggie." Defer any interruptions so you can focus. Then, close your "veggie time" and check your e-mail and voice mail and allow interruptions. Take care of the major matters as quickly as possible. Allow 60 minutes to complete as many requests as possible.

Then, shut out e-mail, phone, and interruptions again and take care of your next-biggest "veggie" for

60 minutes. After you finish it, attend to lower-priority e-mails and phone calls. Get back under control before you go to lunch.

Eat lunch after the people who interrupt you the most; that reduces by an hour or two the time in which they can interrupt you. Also, don't work and eat at the same time; in fact, don't eat lunch at your desk.

By scheduling around your "veggies," batching little tasks (such as phone calls and e-mails), and not letting interruptions and fires control you, you'll be working smarter, not harder. Spend the last 10–15 minutes planning for the following day.

Use your energy cycles to your advantage: We have at least three energy cycles in a day. For 75 percent of us, the strongest is the morning, the next strongest is in the afternoon, and the weakest is in the evening. Work on your difficult tasks in the morning, take the pressure off the afternoon, and reduce the chances you'll have to stay late.

Monday morning is critical: A strong Monday (by working on what matters most because you're fresh from the weekend) makes it more likely that the week will be easier and flow better. Don't schedule meetings or conference calls first thing Monday morning.

Don't overplan daily: We tend to overestimate by 20 percent, on average, the amount of time a task will take. Leave room in your schedule for interruptions, last-minute meetings, and unforeseen problems, so your plan is more realistic and you don't go home frustrated every night.

Finish strong and don't work at night: Don't forget to update your Master List before you go home and try not to sneak in more work after the kids go to bed. If you do, when you get to work the next day, it will feel like you never left and you may pick an easy task, not a "veggie."

Start earlier and leave on time: You can accomplish more before others arrive—and you can spend more time with your family in the evening. Families notice those who come home late more than those who leave early.

Batch like tasks: Set up times each day to return e-mails and phone calls. Turn off your audible e-mail notification.

Make your morning easier: Is your morning (before you get to work) stressful? What could you do the night before that would make your morning a little easier and less stressful?

"I used to look on my list at the end of the day to see what I had left, only to discover that all my work was still left."

☐ ~~Follow your feelings~~

☑ Prioritize requests

The first step in establishing priorities is to improve the information you are receiving when tasks and projects are given to you. It is faster and more accurate to ask questions than to guess or assume the right answer.

The three biggest reasons why people have trouble prioritizing quickly and accurately are:

1. They try to prioritize without the essential information needed. As you will see, the fastest way to improve how you prioritize is to ask better questions.
2. They let human nature get in the way, so they work on what they'd rather work on instead of what they know (deep down) they should work on.
3. They are given very little information at the time the request is made.

Then, you can use the A, B, C method or a decision-making matrix to prioritize tasks.

The A, B, C method is simple:

- An **A** task is one for which *the deadline is today*, and the task is *important to your leader*, offers *visibility for you* and your skills, and is *vital to the needs of your customers, peers, or team members*.
- A **B** task is as important as an A task, but it doesn't have a deadline to be completed today.
- A **C** task is one that you *like* to do, something that you can work on whenever you have some time to spare.

When you prioritize, you must know a task's specific deadline to know the correct *urgency* of the task. When someone gives you a deadline like "ASAP," you must ask, "When do you need it by?"

In order to understand the validity of the deadline, you must ask another question or two to get the reason why the task must be completed by that deadline. When you know the reason for the deadline, you truly know its importance.

To assure that others prioritize your requests correctly, you must give them a specific deadline and explain why you need it by your deadline. To avoid seeming too "pushy," you need to use a cooperative tone when making your request. When you say "ASAP," you give away control of when others will work on your request.

When prioritizing:

Be careful of human nature: Human nature rather than clear thought often affects which task we choose. Some examples are:

- We choose easy tasks before difficult ones.
- We do requests, e-mails, or tasks that don't take a lot of time.
- We work on the new request and drop what we are doing (last in–first out).
- We like to wait to the last minute to start tasks, projects, or goals.
- We start small tasks before large ones.
- We work on other's tasks before our own.
- We choose tasks based on habit, not clear thought.

"The number one reason why people don't prioritize correctly is that they're trying to prioritize without the necessary information—why it's important and when it must be done."

☐ ~~Don't sweat the details~~

☑ Give specific direction

Many times we ask others for information, ask questions, or assign tasks/projects to be completed only to be disappointed when we don't receive a timely answer or the tasks/projects aren't completed on time. Maybe it was your fault. If you had been more specific, maybe that wouldn't have happened. Here is a suggestion:

The four part model to influence others: Instead of saying you want something "ASAP" when you make your next request, try this:

1. **Say to them, "Could you please..."** (to induce cooperation by using the right tone, then engaging them with an open-ended question).

2. **Make your request specific** (to avoid questions).
3. **Give a specific deadline** (to help them prioritize your request).
4. **Mention the consequences if they don't meet your deadline.** (This tells them why your deadline is so important.)

You could also add, "Let me know either way" between step one and two to let them know you are looking for a yes or no followed by a specific time or date by which your request could be completed.

Successful people do one thing at a time: Most people try to do several things at once. Studies show that successful people do only one thing at a time. They realize it will take them less time this way instead of jumping around between tasks. They are able to concentrate better, do the job in less time, and make fewer errors. That is why they often put off interruptions long enough to finish what they're working on.

Note: If you have to give up what you're currently working on to work on the new task or request, be sure you create a "mental bridge" back to what you were working on when the interruption occurred. Make some notes or reminders about what you were thinking about at the time of the interruption and be sure you put it back on your list before you jump to the new task.

When negotiating requests, write down the task and deadline: Your word is your bond. Write down their request immediately and circle the deadline, so you don't forget to deliver on time or early.

Know what's important to your leader: That should help you prioritize, if you cannot decide by evaluating tasks in terms of goals. It's faster and more accurate to ask your leader questions and be 100 percent right than to guess and be wrong. Show your boss and others what you already have on your list.

Your boss may delegate the task to someone else. If you are giving tasks to your direct reports, be sure to ask to see their Master Lists, so you can try to spread the work more evenly among all your direct reports.

"The number one reason why people don't prioritize correctly is that they're trying to prioritize without the necessary information—why it's important and what the deadline is."

☐ **Work longer hours**

☑ **Find more time for you**

If you want to get all of your work done so you can go home two hours earlier, you have to eliminate two hours' worth of activities. You won't find all two hours in one place; it will be more like five minutes here and 10 minutes there.

Start by examining how you're spending your time. Look at the tasks on your Master List and your Daily List, and consider all unscheduled tasks.

For each, ask these two questions:

■ Was this the best use of my time?
■ Was I doing the right task at the right time?

You should categorize the tasks that you handled:

■ Which could have been eliminated?

- Which could have taken less of my time?
- Which could I have delegated?
- Which could I have batched with similar tasks?

This analysis should suggest ways to manage your time better in the future. How could you plan, organize, and prioritize better? Are you working on everything but the right task? Try to be painstakingly honest about what you could improve.

The key for most people is to start with the morning. If you're a morning person, that's where you can make the greatest productivity gains. If not, then look at the afternoon. The early afternoon is best; it's generally a mistake to leave important tasks until the late afternoon or to try to do them after hours. About 90 percent of all productivity gains typically occur in the first part of your day.

How could you set up each day so you could start faster, work with more discipline, and get more done in the morning? Organize before you leave work rather than when you arrive. Minimize the time you spend "relationship building" the first thing in the morning.

Here are four recommendations for finding time:

Anticipate problems: Schedule realistically, aware of things that might go wrong, rather than optimistically. You're more likely to do tasks right and not waste time as problems surprise you.

Protect your "veggie" time: You should have two "power hours" every day. I recommend the morning, as I outlined in the lesson "Plan for Power." This is when you should do your "veggies."

Prevent and limit interruptions: The biggest problem productivity killer people encounter today is the sheer number of interruptions they face in the form of e-mails, phone calls, and face-to-face visitors. If you could save two to ten minutes on each interruption you get, that could save you up to 120 minutes a day, or two hours.

Batch similar activities when possible: It may be more efficient to handle (read and write) e-mail, answer voice mail, and make other phone calls in chunks of time—15 minutes as a break or an hour between bigger tasks.

"We shall never have more time. We have, and we have always had, all the time there is."
—Arnold Bennett

☐ Work now, organize ~~later~~

☑ Control your desk

When our desks are cluttered, we lose in at least three ways. We lose 45 minutes every day, on average, hunting for things on our desks, going through papers and notes. When our desks are cluttered, we lose focus as well as time.

Here are some easy steps to gain control of your desk:

Think of yourself as a jukebox. A jukebox takes out a CD, plays the selected song or songs, and then puts it back. Then it gets another. It doesn't stack the CDs on each other. Get the point? It increases focus and concentration only having one file in front of you at a time.

You won't take the piles off your desk until you can:

- Keep the task or tasks you need to complete in each file in front of your eyes by using a Master List or calendar.
- Find your files quickly in your file drawer.

Here are some easy steps to gain control of your desk.

- *Take everything off your desk.* In other words, "zero-base" your desktop. Wipe it clean for a fresh beginning, like you're just moving in. Then, put things back in the order in which you use them most. What can you do without? Throw away outdated items, put your pictures behind you or to the side. Toss out any candy: it attracts visitors.

- *Put a clock where it will keep you aware of time.* Your perception of time and the reality of it are often different. A watch on the wrist and a time display on the computer are not enough. Put your clock in-between your two biggest interrupters, the phone and computer (e-mail).

- *Organize your tools.* Empty your desk. Cut down on pens, pencils, paper clips, and so forth; try to put them all into one drawer. Keep just a month's supply of stationery. Divide your drawers into separate areas for stationery, files, personal things, etc. Toss any extra stuff you don't really need.

Your papers and files should be broken down into three categories:

- The future (someday I'd like to read or start working on).
- The past (you've already finished it).
- The present (it's something you're currently working on).

Only worry about catching up the present first, it's the highest priority. That goes for e-mail too. File your most recent e-mails first and work backward.

Keep only the "present" in your desk file: The best way to overcome paper overload is to manage only the present—what you're working on now and for the next four weeks. You'll focus on organizing the present first.

Set aside the past: Remove from your desk file all files that have been completed or closed out and put them on the floor for the time being. Since you'll only be using them for reference we will file them last.

Set aside the future: Remove from your desk file anything that you expect to be needing or reading in the future. This too will be filed for reference after you have finished filing the present.

"Order is the best manager of Time; for unless work is properly arranged, Time is lost."

—Samuel Smiles

☐ ~~Organize occasionally~~

☑ Manage your desk

Now that you've removed the clutter from your desktop and drawers, you're ready to establish a new order.

Organize the present first: Don't worry about the future or the past until you've organized everything else.

Set up your working files in your desk drawer(s) or within arm's length. Organize them alphabetically or chronologically, whichever makes more sense for you.

Limit the categories by keeping them broad: Set up no more than seven to ten; if you have more, it will take longer to find a file. I'd suggest files for "fingertip info" (phone lists, addresses, and information you use frequently), current projects (a file for each project), routine tasks, clients or prospects, and problems or issues to be researched.

Don't put too many papers in a file or it will take longer to find what you want. Split big files into smaller files for greater convenience. Get honest about what you really need and what you should toss.

As you name each file, think about how you would try to find it later. Make your file names interesting, but logical. Keep them short—not more than three words.

Write them in large letters with a bold, fine-tip marking pen to make the files easy to find.

Use colored file folders to distinguish among your categories so you can find files faster.

Now you are ready to put the piles away that you originally put on the floor when you started. Break your piles into small piles because you are going to file one small pile a day, at the end of the day, until you get caught up. That way you won't procrastinate starting.

Handle paper only once: Once you touch a file or piece of paper in one of your stacks, it can't go back where it came from. It must go in one of the five following places:

- The garbage
- The future
- The past
- The present
- Outbound (sign off on it, or delegate it to someone else)

That file or piece of paper can't be placed back on your desk. (Many times, that's why our piles don't get smaller. The paper just goes back into a new pile on our desk.) These five options eliminate questions and the need for new piles.

Stop using post-its: Stop using sticky notes for to-do items. They only create clutter and increase the amount of time it takes to find your notes. Take all your post-its, write them on your Master List, and throw them away.

Finally, put the future and the past into the reference file. This is a file cabinet that should be located in a corner of your office or just outside.

File a little every day: If you do, the situation won't get out of hand again. Toss what you don't need. Every Friday, go through your files and get rid of any duplicates or ones you no longer need.

Clean your desk every day: Put your files away. You'll feel more in control—both as you leave and when you arrive. And you won't be worrying about leaving sensitive papers exposed—or any files vulnerable to damage if the sprinklers go off while you're away.

"Order is most useful in the management of everything . . . Its maxim is: A place for everything, and everything in its place."

—Samuel Smiles

☐ ~~Be available always~~

☑ Limit interruptions

The average interruption takes six to nine minutes and requires four to five additional minutes for recovery. After three or four interruptions, your focus and concentration will be gone. Interruptions can take time and affect your focus.

To gain control over your interruptions, every time you get interrupted ask yourself, "Is this truly something I must handle right away?" That will really put your interruptions into perspective. You'll find out after you hear what they need that many don't need immediate attention.

Evaluate each interruption to determine if it is a "veggie":

■ Does it relate to one of your goals, priorities, or key projects?

■ Is the request important to the needs of a customer, a peer, or a team member?

■ Is it something time-sensitive from your team leader or boss?

Reduce the noise around you: Noise is one of the fastest ways to lose focus, making it very difficult to be productive. Do people like to congregate outside your cubicle? Have a team agreement that it's okay to tell each other (without feeling bad) to please keep it down or to use a conference or break room. Don't be afraid to say something.

Take chairs out of your office: Discourage visitors from staying by removing extra chairs or putting files on them. Visitors will tire of standing and leave.

Put a sign on your door or cubicle: Put a picture of a "veggie" on your door, or a schedule with times when you will and won't be available, and a note pad so that people can leave their requests in writing instead of disturbing you.

Have a "selective" open door policy: If possible, keep your door closed during your "veggie" times. Announce and post hours when you'll be available. Set specific times for people who report to you—and promise not to touch the phone or e-mail while they're with you. If you can't close your door, escape to a vacant office or meeting room. Tell as few people as possible where you are.

Manager's tip: Try to get out of your office at least twice each morning to ask your team members if they have any questions or need anything. You'll be more visible and they'll have less need to come to your office.

Delegate the interruption to the right person: If you're not the right person to answer a question or solve a problem, don't try to please: delegate the interruption to the appropriate person.

Stand up to limit the interruption: The best way to send a clear message that you don't have a lot of time is to stand up when a visitor arrives. Don't sit down. Avoid getting into a conversation.

Arrange a later time: Offer to meet later, to discuss the matter without distractions. Be sure to go see them so you can limit the amount of time the interruption takes.

Block off time on your computer: Schedule time on your computer to get your "veggies" done. If you don't block off time on your computer, the next thing you know you will be in meetings all day long.

Respect others: Before interrupting someone, always ask, "Do you have a minute?" Ask others to do the same with you.

Set up a group "power hour": At your next team meeting, suggest designating certain times when interruptions and noise are to be minimized. Everyone on the team agrees not to interrupt each other and to try to get a "veggie" done in that hour. Schedule your "power hour" in the morning.

"Always evaluate your interruptions. Ask yourself, 'Is this something I must handle now?'"

☐ ~~Let your e-mail~~
~~manage you~~

☑ **Manage your e-mail**

E-mails can be especially efficient for requesting information, providing requested information, conveying information, exchanges that should be documented, and communicating with more than one person at a time. But remember: e-mail is technically devoid of tone. It's whatever the reader thinks you meant when he or she opens your e-mail message.

The phone is better when a response is needed immediately, when voices and tones are important to the message, when there's something to discuss, and when privacy is needed.

Set up convenient times to check e-mail: Turn off the notification feature so it doesn't distract you and interrupt your work. Tell people that if they have time-sensitive questions or requests that need a reaction within an hour to call you instead. Remember, if it goes "ding" you will check it and try to do something about it.

Only look for "veggies" the first thing daily:
Compare new messages with the half-dozen "veggies" that you put on your Daily List the evening before to decide whether a task is a "veggie" or not.

Use the auto preview function: That way you can quickly read the subject line and first three or four lines of the message. After checking your e-mail, set the view to normal.

Set up effective folders: Set up folders to save messages you want to keep, such as "take action immediately," "pending," "fingertip reference," "meetings," "delegate," and "projects." Within each, set up subfolders. Your e-mail folders and subfolders should match your desk filing system. Don't have too many or you won't be able to find anything anyway.

Don't use your in-box as a to-do list: It's like piling papers on your desk. Never have more than one screen of e-mail messages in your in-box. Set up a reminder for the messages you file. Move messages to your calendar as appropriate.

Act on e-mails when you read them the first time. Go through all the messages once and delete spam and other wastes of time. Then, act on the most important messages. Finally, file the rest to keep your in-box clean and save time. At the end of each day and week set up times to delete and file e-mail so it doesn't get out of hand.

Use "rules" to manage your e-mail: Create filters or rules to block, delete, or route incoming messages directly into the appropriate file folder that you specify. Also, get yourself removed from electronic mailing lists unless you really need them.

Batch your responses to e-mail: When you are doing one thing at a time, it will take less time. By checking your e-mail at regular intervals (say, four times a day), you can concentrate on handling just your e-mail and finish faster. Give yourself 15–30 minutes to handle as many messages in your in-box as you can, in the correct priority, then close it and work on something else.

Use the "out-of-office" feature: Use your e-mail like you would your voice mail. If you're going to be out of the office, adjust your sender's expectation of a quick response by setting up the Out of Office feature. This will tell your sender immediately that you're out of the office for a specific period, so they can contact someone else in your place until you return.

Reply promptly: Return e-mails the same day. At least acknowledge receipt; otherwise, the sender may call or e-mail until you do. Tell the sender if you'll be away; use the "out-of-office" feature to reply to each e-mail.

"E-mail is the most abused form of communication in the workplace today."

□ ~~Type and send~~, then think

☑ **Master outgoing e-mail**

Write e-mails so you get better results faster. The average person decides in five to ten seconds whether to take action, file, or delete an e-mail. Recipients want to know three things:

- Why did I get this e-mail?
- What do I have to do?
- When do you need it?

Identify what the purpose of your e-mail is: Before you begin writing, determine the purpose of your e-mail and make a bulleted list of what you need or want to discuss. This will help keep your message short, to the point, and help you write the appropriate subject line.

Use your subject line more effectively: Try to get the reader's attention by writing a specific subject line using approximately six words to get them to react appropriately. Put the purpose of your e-mail in the form of a phrase (not one word), in the subject line. If your e-mail is time sensitive, put your deadline in the subject line so it stands out.

Make your e-mail look easy: People tend to handle first any e-mails that look easy or quick. Make your first paragraph no longer than two or three lines. Keep your message short—a few paragraphs—if possible. Don't write in long paragraphs. Use numbers and bullets to invite your reader to read your e-mail and take action.

If your e-mail is going to be more than one screen include an attachment.

This will make your e-mail look easy, like a fax cover sheet. Your e-mail will then give the reader direction regarding the attachment.

Motivate your reader to respond: Always try to finish your e-mail with a deadline, in the form of a question, and your reason for the deadline or the consequences if they don't respond. This will help them prioritize your e-mail. Don't use ASAP or thank you in advance to get them to respond. Mark your e-mail as urgent only if it's really urgent.

Example: "Could you please return your time cards by this Friday so you can be paid next week?"

Create a signature to help recipients: Provide alternative ways for people to contact you. It should include your mailing address and phone number. Keep it to six lines or fewer.

Give instructions with forwards: If you must forward a message, put your comments at the top, either in the subject line or the first paragraph. This saves the recipient time and gets better results. "FYI" doesn't really tell the recipient anything.

Always review each message before you send it: Make sure it's complete, concise, and organized logically. Verify the grammar and spelling. Set up spell check to help catch mistakes—but don't trust it to do the job for you.

E-mail etiquette: Write e-mail messages as if they were letters or memos. Don't use shortcuts or symbols. Don't type in all caps or all lower case. Use simple formats and avoid fancy backgrounds. Your style and language should be appropriate to your knowledge of the recipient and/or the subject. Don't write anything that you wouldn't say in person. E-mail is admissible in a court of law, so use the phone if the matter is sensitive.

"Consider carefully what you write and who may read it eventually. If the president of your company received your e-mail, what would he or she think?"

☐ ~~Let your phone manage you~~

☑ Manage incoming calls

Phone calls undermine time management. Many are unnecessary or take longer than necessary. Reduce the calls you take and the time they take from you.

Keep a phone log for a week: Note the time, the caller's name, the purpose of the call, and the duration. Then, evaluate your log. Which calls were absolutely necessary? Could you have delegated any? How can you reduce your time on each call?

Screen your calls: At least during your "veggie time," screen your calls if it's not necessary for you to answer every call. If you have an assistant, first thing in the morning provide and explain your schedule so he or she knows how to prioritize callers. If you don't have an assistant, use voice mail.

Assess the call quickly: If you answer a call, ask, "What can I do for you?" Encourage the caller to get to the point quickly. Ask questions until you determine the purpose of the call.

Then, decide how the call relates to your priorities. Is it worth interrupting your current task to handle immediately? Can you call the person back at a time that fits your schedule and is appropriate to the priority of the call?

Delegate the call to the right person: If someone else could handle the call better, either because it's low priority or because you don't have the information, provide the name and number of the person who can help or offer to forward the call to that person.

Use voice mail more effectively:

- Change your greeting daily or at least weekly, to give your schedule for that day or that week.
- Ask callers to please leave their name, number, reason for the call, and the best time to call back. (Explain that doing so will enable you to call back sooner with the desired help or information.)
- Provide options: another phone number or a pager number for reaching you, the name and

number of another person to call, and voice mail.

Three suggestions for managing incoming calls:

Let people know the best time to reach you: Let people know the best times and the times to avoid if they need to reach you by phone. Also, provide the names and numbers of any coworkers whom they can call instead.

When you leave voice mail for others: Try to leave a detailed voice mail in the same way you're asking them to do for you. This is why I plan my call before I pick up the phone. Give them a deadline by which to respond if possible (not ASAP). Be sure to speak slowly, especially when leaving your phone number, so they can write it down!

Leave your phone number twice in the message: Once at the beginning and once at the end of the message. Don't leave messages longer than thirty seconds, if possible.

"On the average, one out of every two business calls is not about business. The telephone is an interruption. You stop your work when it rings . . . , so you have to learn how to manage it."

☐ ~~Call and talk, then plan~~

☑ Master outgoing calls

Prioritize your calls. Then try to figure out the best time to call—and if you need to talk with a person. Here are some suggestions for saving time on every call you have to make:

Plan every call before you pick up the phone: That's the smartest way to save time on calls you make. Write down the points to cover and prepare all necessary information. Know how long you expect to take for your points. Keep the call focused.

Anticipate any questions they might have: The other person is likely to ask and prepare an answer, along with any information needed. You'll seem more professional and save time.

Keep your call focused: Check the time before calling and then keep track while you're on the phone. Specifically:

- Start by giving your reason(s) for calling—and then mention your key points in order of importance and stick with them.
- When you've achieved the goal(s) of your call, politely end the call.
- Summarize the call and ask, "Does that cover everything?" Then, my favorite, say, "I know you're really busy, so I'm going to let you go."

Make telephone appointments: If the other person is too busy to talk, make an appointment to call back. Write it down—and make sure that the other person writes it down, too.

By planning your call before you pick up the phone, you will be better prepared to leave a short, specific message with a deadline for them to call you back if appropriate. When you leave a voice mail, keep your message short—15 to 30 seconds; otherwise they won't call you back. Speak slowly and clearly.

Here are four more suggestions for making phone calls:

Set aside specific times to make calls: Batch your calls so they take less time. Make the most important calls in the morning. Batch lower-priority calls from 11:30 a.m. to noon and at the end of the day. People are quicker on the phone before lunch and before they're leaving for the day. Return all voice mail messages within 24 hours, the same day if possible.

Make notes on your Master List: When you talk on the phone, keep track, especially of agreements and commitments, for future reference.

Choose voice mail if possible: If someone offers to take a message, ask for voice mail so you can leave a more detailed message and it will get through accurately: "It would probably be easier for you if I could leave a voice mail message."

Return all calls from salespeople: Leave a message that you're not interested or you'll call if interested. This should eliminate future calls from those people—a good investment of a few seconds.

If you're calling to provide or request information and don't need to speak with the other person, try to pick a time when he or she won't be there, so you can just leave a message.

"On average, an unplanned phone call takes five minutes longer than one that has been planned. Planning a phone call can be as easy as a 30-second outline of what you want to say or ask."
—Gary Lockwood

☐ ~~Do it all yourself~~

☑ Delegate

Delegation is a very effective means of time management.

Unfortunately, many of us don't do it enough.

There are compelling benefits when you successfully delegate. The benefits of delegation include:

- It will save you an amazing amount of time.
- It is one of the highest forms of motivation known because it encourages participation.
- It develops your staff into a more productive group.
- It encourages trust and cooperation on your team.
- It increases the level of teamwork for your direct reports.
- It improves your skills (at training, coaching, and mentoring).

Before you begin, make a list of all the tasks for which you're currently responsible. Then decide which tasks or projects will benefit the company or division (tasks that mean something), will improve your abilities or performance, or will benefit a subordinate's knowledge and confidence. Now select one.

Choose the right person for the job: Make sure that the person you select has the proper training, experience, and/or knowledge for the job. Tell why you've chosen him or her and why you've assigned this particular task.

Define the task, your desired results, and your expectations: Provide guidelines and examples of what's expected, as appropriate. Be sure the designee understands your desired outcome *before* beginning. There are no silly questions at the beginning.

Set a start time and a deadline: Allow sufficient time for him or her to complete the task or project. Schedule a meeting midway between the start and end time to discuss progress or other issues, but don't hover or keep checking with the person every five minutes. Give him or her some room to learn.

Make sure the designee has the proper training: The number one reason why delegation often fails is that the person delegating does not have time to train the designee. Make the time to train! If you take the time, you'll only have to train once and the task will be done right the first time.

I typically like to pick the afternoon to train because it's less hectic, I've finished what I wanted to that day, and it's easier to avoid interruptions.

TIP: If it's a report, explain how it should be done (even if you could have done it in the same amount of time yourself), and let the person keep a copy of it.

Give them the necessary authority: Make sure your designee has the necessary authority to gain access to certain files or to get cooperation from others. Send an e-mail message in advance on behalf of your designee to those whose cooperation will be needed so things will run more smoothly.

Give praise or feedback at the end: At the conclusion of the job, discuss the results with the person. Praise him or her for the results, discuss any issues, and offer constructive feedback.

Track the tasks: Use your calendar or your Master List to keep track of the tasks you're delegating. Remember, you are the one ultimately responsible for the success or failure of the task or project.

"There is a great man who makes every man feel small. But the really great man makes every man feel great."

—Chinese proverb

☐ ~~Meet: it's good for business~~

☑ **Plan meetings smartly**

We are all familiar with the characteristics of unproductive meetings. They are longer, and more of them are needed. We can start improving meetings by planning smartly. Ask, is this meeting really necessary? That's the first and most important question. Why meet? There are three basic purposes for meetings: to provide information, to solve problems or make decisions, and to brainstorm.

Calculate the cost of a meeting. Is it possible to serve your purpose in another way? Consider alternatives. For example, if your purpose is to convey information, such as news and reports, maybe e-mail would be better.

Meet only if there's a reason. That may seem obvious, but many meetings are "regular meetings"—every week or even every day—same time, same place, same old.... Regularity is not a reason for meeting.

Define your desired outcome: If you decide that a meeting is needed, you should also decide the length and timing of the meeting and whom to invite, how long it should take, and when to schedule it.

Tell people why they've been invited: Include in the meeting *only* people who need to be there. Then, tell each participant why you're including him or her and what you're expecting from each of them. As a result, participants will take greater responsibility in preparing and participating.

Ask participants to submit topics for the agenda: Get everyone involved. Your participants can often provide ideas you never thought of. This will give them a stake in the meeting and increase the probability that they will show up on time or early.

Limit the objectives of your meeting: Short, to-the-point meetings are the most effective. Try to limit your meeting to one hour or less! The average person's attention span is 60–90 minutes, yet the clear majority of meetings are longer than 90 minutes.

Determine the points to cover, how you will handle each, and how long each issue, main point, or topic should take. The next time you make your agenda, eliminate the lowest 20 percent of your agenda, and you might finish on time or early.

Have an agenda and distribute it early: A meeting without an agenda is a tip-off that the meeting is going to be a "bull session" and will run past its end time. Get your agenda out at least 24 hours ahead of time to give everyone plenty of time to organize their schedules so they can attend your meeting.

Use the "veggie" principle to organize your agenda: Cover the most important items on your agenda first. That way, if people are called away or you run out of time, it won't matter as much because the important items on the agenda have already been covered. This will really help you finish the meeting on time.

Have a strict start and end time for your meeting: Make sure everyone understands the meeting is going to start on time and close the door at that specified time. Teach others to be respectful of your time and do the same for them in turn. Also, make sure your meeting finishes on time or allow them to leave if they have another commitment to get to.

When to schedule meetings: The purpose of the meeting dictates when to schedule it. Unless you are brainstorming on trying to make an important decision, try to schedule your meeting in the afternoon. Only schedule a morning meeting if it's a "Veggie" where you need all of your participants "fresh." Schedule staff meetings on Mondays, not Fridays, and avoid any same-day meeting.

"There is no best time to schedule an unnecessary meeting."

—Anonymous

☐ ~~Gather and go~~

☑ Run smart meetings

You've planned and scheduled the meeting smartly. Now, run it smartly. Write the meeting objectives on a white board or a flipchart at the front of the room, so that meeting participants will be focused as soon as they arrive.

Have ground rules: Let your participants set and agree to ground rules that will give your meeting the appropriate standards and structure. This will help you keep control of your meeting and reduce the chances of interruptions, sidebar issues, or discussions of issues not on your agenda. Some examples of ground rules are:

- Turn off cell phones, Blackberries, and so on.
- Don't bring other work to the meeting.
- Go for focus, momentum, and achieving your objective.
- Don't cancel at the last minute (you must send someone in your place).
- Everyone should be prepared to share.

- Everyone's opinion matters.
- Everyone is to be treated with respect.

Get to the room early: That way you can set up the meeting room the way you want it, get your PowerPoint ready, and greet participants as they arrive. This will show that you are serious about getting results and that you respect their time.

Set the tone from the beginning: Show participants that you value their time by thanking them at the beginning for coming to your meeting on time. Everyone likes a little appreciation.

Get everyone involved from the beginning: Go around the room and ask everyone to say their name, department, why they are there, and what they want to get out of the meeting. The sooner you get everyone involved the better the sharing will be.

By getting people to share quickly, you can get a read on how quiet or how outspoken they are and their level of enthusiasm for being at your meeting. Make sure everyone shares by calling on them.

Cover only the topics on the agenda: The number one reason why meetings don't finish on time is that the leader of the meeting loses control of the meeting. Be the Ringmaster so that the meeting sticks to the agenda! A meeting that sticks to the agenda will finish faster, and the next time you schedule a meeting, people will be far more likely to attend. It also presents an organized and professional image.

Use a flipchart to engage and control your group:
If other issues come up, write them down on a flipchart; and if there's time at the end of the meeting, you can discuss them. Otherwise, you can save them for the next meeting.

Keep minutes: The person responsible should include the "formal stuff" (date, time, leader, purpose, participants), then record key points that relate to the agenda, and then ask questions to clarify any contributions or decisions.

Generate ideas, build consensus, and stay neutral:
You must remain impartial and guide participants to share their thoughts, ideas, and opinions. You need to set up a "safe" environment where participants feel safe to contribute their ideas.

If you don't think you can do this either appoint an impartial facilitator or try to work out a solution. If a participant objects to a decision it is important to find out why and work through their objection. To have a consensus you must consider all concerns and find the most agreeable course of action.

"Nobody knows when the first meeting took place, but it's a safe bet that the meeting seemed too long to some participants, poorly organized to others, and boring to at least a few, and it's likely that some were disappointed in the results."
—Barbara J. Streibel

☐ ~~Just let the meeting~~
~~ramble~~

☑ **Close and execute**

You need to do everything possible to make sure your meeting met its objective. Hopefully you had a limited objective when you scheduled the meeting. Be sure before everyone leaves the meeting to:

Ask each participant for recommendations: Don't just agree to schedule another meeting. Make sure that you have made significant progress towards a solution or meeting the objective of your meeting. Go around the room and ask each person for final recommendations before the meeting ends. Try to narrow the solution to no more than two.

Be sure you summarize the main points of the meeting, any decisions the group made, action items for the next meeting, and assignments for participants.

Give participants assignments for the next meeting: Make sure you give out action items before the meeting ends. Make sure each participant understands what is expected of him/her for the next meeting. Write them down. Write a follow-up e-mail so they know what they'll be responsible for preparing for the next meeting. Action items that aren't written down usually don't get done!

Thank everyone for their time and input: Showing verbal appreciation at the end of a meeting shows participants that you value their time and the sacrifice they made to be there. It can go a long way toward getting them to come again.

Make sure the meeting finishes on time: If you prioritized your agenda properly (by discussing the most important issue first) you should be down to the lesser items on your agenda by the time your meeting is supposed to end.

People are more likely to accept a meeting invitation from a person that finishes a meeting on time or early than someone that constantly allows their meeting to run past the allotted time.

Distribute the meeting minutes: The job of the note taker is to get the notes from the meeting finalized and distributed to all of the participants within 24 hours (either in writing or by e-mail). They should be finalized and distributed quickly while the meeting is still "fresh" on everyone's mind and so participants can confirm the notes or ask questions so everyone is on the same page.

"A meeting without a leader, an agenda, or minutes has a high probability of accomplishing nothing and being a 'bull session' in disguise."

–An anonymous meeting participant

"Time waste differs from material waste in that there can be no salvage. The easiest of all wastes and the hardest to correct is the waste of time, because wasted time does not litter the floor like wasted material."

—Henry Ford

"It is better to underpromise and overdeliver than to overpromise and underdeliver!"

The McGraw-Hill Mighty Managers Handbooks

The Powell Principles
by Oren Harari (0-07-144490-4)

> Details two dozen mission- and people-based leadership skills that have guided Colin Powell through his nearly half-century of service to the United States.

> Provides a straight-to-the-point guide that any leader in any arena can follow for unmitigated success.

How Buffett Does It
by James Pardoe (0-07-144912-4)

> Expands on 24 primary ideas Warren Buffett has followed from day one.

> Reveals Buffett's stubborn adherence to the time-honored fundamentals of value investing.

The Lombardi Rules
by Vince Lombardi, Jr. (0-07-144489-0)

> Presents more than two dozen of the tenets and guidelines Lombardi used to drive him and those around him to unprecedented levels of success.

> Packed with proven insights and techniques that are especially valuable in today's turbulent business world.

The Welch Way

by Jeffrey A. Krames (0-07-142953-0)

> Draws on the career of Jack Welch to explain how workers can follow his proven model.

> Shows how to reach new heights in today's wide-open, idea-driven workplace.

The Ghosn Factor

by Miguel Rivas-Micoud (0-07-148595-3)

> Examines the life, works, and words of Carlos Ghosn, CEO of *Nissan* and *Renault*.

> Provides 24 succinct lessons that managers can immediately apply.

How to Motivate Every Employee

by Anne Bruce (0-07-146330-5)

> Provides strategies for infusing your employees with a passion for the work they do.

> Packed with techniques, tips, and suggestions that are proven to motivate in all industries and environments.

The New Manager's Handbook

by Morey Stettner (0-07-146332-1)

> Gives tips for teaming with your employees to achieve extraordinary goals.

> Outlines field-proven techniques to succeed and win the respect of both your employees and your supervisors.

The Sales Success Handbook

by Linda Richardson (0-07-146331-3)

> Shows how to sell customers—not by what you tell them, but by how well you listen to what they have to say.

> Explains how to persuasively position the value you bring to meet the customer's business needs.

How to Plan and Execute Strategy

by Wallace Stettinius, D. Robley Wood, Jr., Jacqueline L. Doyle, and John L. Colley, Jr. (0-07-148437-X)

> Provides 24 practical steps for devising, implementing, and managing market-defining, growth-driving strategies.

> Outlines a field-proven framework that can be followed to strengthen your company's competitive edge.

How to Manage Performance

by Robert Bacal (0-07-148439-8)

> Provides goal-focused, common-sense techniques to stimulate employee productivity in any environment.

> Details how to align employee goals and set performance incentives.

Managing in Times of Change

by Michael D. Maginn (0-07-148436-1)

> Helps you to understand and explain the benefits of change, while flourishing within the new environment.

> Provides straight talk and actionable advice for teams, managers, and individuals.

Leadership When the Heat Is On

by Danny Cox with John Hoover (0-07-148653-4)

Provides 24 practical lessons in high-performance management when under pressure.

Hands-on techniques for infusing your company with results-driven leadership during times of mergers, layoffs, and other organizational turmoil.

About the Author

Kenneth Zeigler is a top expert on time management, organization, and productivity improvement. He has authored many articles on these subjects, and he was the first author to discover the problem is not the system people use but rather their organization skill set.

Ken has served in senior management at firms such as Pillsbury, Hughes, Quaker Oats, Merrill Lynch, and Dean Witter. As a consultant he has advised clients such as Hertz, Hormel, the Federal Reserve, the Comptroller of the Currency, and Fidelity.

Ken attended the University of Minnesota as an undergraduate, where he was a member of the varsity football team, and then completed graduate work in advertising and finance at the University of Illinois. He lives in Nashville with his wife, Mary Beth, and his sons, Zachary and Nicholas.

Visit his Web site at www.kztraining.com.